...But Noah found grace in the eyes of the Lord.

Other books by Peter Spier

The Fox Went Out on a Chilly Night
London Bridge Is Falling Down!
To Market! To Market!
Hurrah, We're Outward Bound!
And So My Garden Grows
Of Dikes and Windmills
The Erie Canal
Gobble, Growl, Grunt
Crash! Bang! Boom!
Fast-slow, High-low
The Star-Spangled Banner
Tin Lizzie

NOAH'S ARK

Published by Bantam Doubleday Dell Books for Young Readers,
a division of Bantam Doubleday Dell Publishing Group, Inc.
1540 Broadway, New York, New York 10036

The trademarks Yearling® and Dell® are registered in the U.S. Patent
and Trademark Office and in other countries.

ISBN: 0-440-40693-5

Reprinted by arrangement with Doubleday Books for Young Readers

Printed in the United States of America
September 1992
10 9 8 7 6
OAN

NOAH'S ARK

Illustrated by Peter Spier

A PICTURE YEARLING BOOK

The Flood
Jacobus Revius (1586–1658)
Translated from the Dutch by Peter Spier

High and long,
Thick and strong,
Wide and stark,
Was the ark.
Climb on board,
Said the Lord.
Noah's kin
Clambered in.
Cow and moose,
Hare and goose,
Sheep and ox,
Bee and fox,
Stag and doe,
Elk and crow,
Lynx and bear,
All were there.
Stork and frog,
Skunk and hog,
Ape and snail,
Stoat and quail,

Flea and hound,
Could be found.
Lark and wren,
Hawk and hen,
Finch and kite,
Flew inside.
Dog and cat,
Mouse and rat,
Fly and vole,
Worm and mole,
Creatures all,
Large and small,
Good and mean,
Foul and clean,
Fierce and tame,
In they came,
Pair by pair,
Gross and fair.
All that walked,
Crawled or stalked

On dry earth
Found a berth.
But the rest,
Worst and best,
Stayed on shore,
Were no more.
That whole host
Gave the ghost.
They were killed
For the guilt
Which brought all
To the Fall.
Later on
It was done:
Back on land
Through God's hand,
Who forgave,
And did save.
The Lord's Grace
Be the praise!

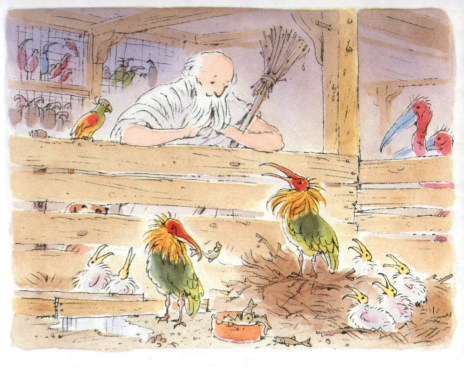

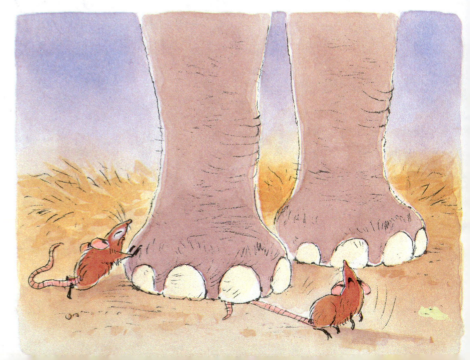

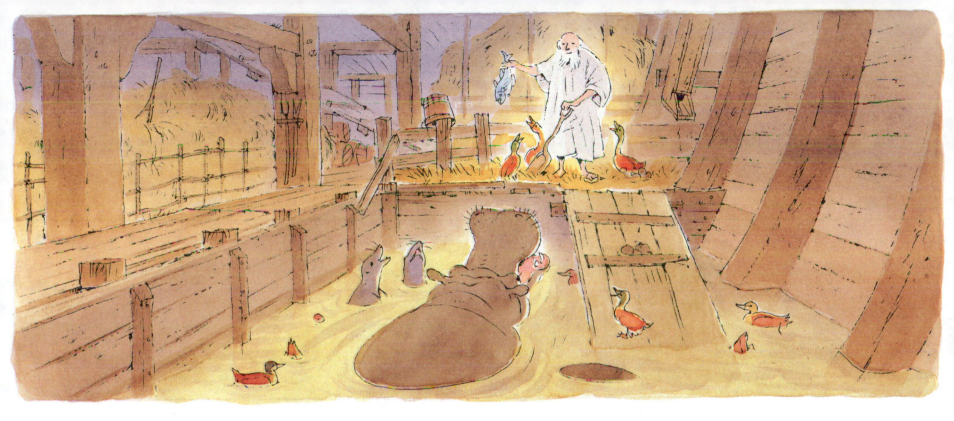

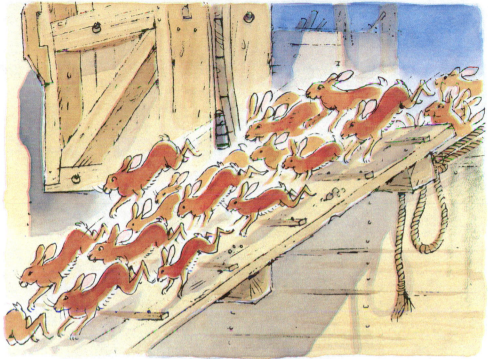
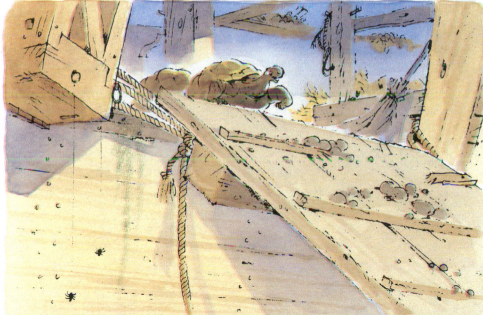

... and he planted a vineyard.